THE BEANO

SUMMER BUMPER

Parragon
Bath · New York · Singapore · Hong Kong · Cologne · Delhi · Melbourne

Beano books

First published under license by Parragon in 2007
Parragon
Queen Street House
4 Queen Street
Bath BA1 1HE, UK

ISBN 978-1-4054-9732-9

Printed in China

INTRODUCTION

This Beano Summer Bumper will keep you entertained for hours and hours! Dennis, Gnasher, Minnie, Walter, the Bash Street Kids, Roger the Dodger and the rest of your favourites are all inside. Laugh milk out your nose as you read the hilarious jokes and riddles, then strain your brain as you do the awesome activities and puzzles!

What's the difference between HOMEWORK and BREAKFAST?

Gnasher didn't eat Dennis's Breakfast!

Why did Curly eat Dennis's homework?

Because Gnasher wasn't hungry!

What's yellow and dangerous?

Shark infested custard!

What's green and dangerous?

An angry lettuce!

What's yellow, green and brown and dangerous?

A three-week old cheese sandwich!

TOMATO THROWING

Dennis is trying to find some tomatoes to throw at Softy Walter. Can you help Dennis find the right route?

TOTALLY TRICKY MATHS

Try to arrange five odd numbers into a sum that will add to fourteen.

ANSWER: 11+1+1+1=14

What's the last thing that goes through a fly's mind when it hits a windscreen?

Its **bottom!**

How do you know which end of a worm is its head?

Wait for it to burp!

What has 20 feet and sounds awful?

The school choir!

What has a Q
and lots of Ps
and smells awful?
School dinners!

GIRLS' NAMES

Print a girl's name in the empty boxes reading across to complete seven girls' names reading downwards.

	A		C		
	L	A	O	L	P
A	C	N	N	N	A
R	E	E	I	D	R
Y			E	A	L

NSWER: Minnie

CHANGING OF THE WIND

Change 'wind' to 'calm' in 5 moves, changing one letter at each turn, to form a new word.

ANSWER: wind, wild, will, wall, call, calm is one solution

What
do you call
a boy who likes
rolling in leaves?

Russell!

What
do you call
a boy who likes
floating in the sea?

BOB!

HOW MANY SOFTIES DOES IT TAKE TO CHANGE A LIGHT BULB?

NONE.
Softies don't change light bulbs, they get their mumsies to do it for them!

HOW MANY GNASHERS DOES IT TAKE TO CHANGE A LIGHT BULB?

NONE.
Who do you think broke it in the first place?

WATER WORDS

Change one letter in each of the words below to spell six bodies of water.

1. PONY
2. CREEP
3. FOOL
4. SEW
5. LAME
6. LIVER

ANSWERS: 1. Pond, 2. Creek, 3. Pool, 4. Sea, 5. Lake, 6. River

WHAT DO YOU GET IF YOU DIAL 666?

THE AUSTRALIAN POLICE!

WHAT DO YOU GET IF YOU DIAL 333?

HALF THE AUSTRALIAN POLICE!

WHAT DO YOU GET IF YOU DIAL 01245-2846-5598-6083-0977?

A VERY SORE FINGER!

What do you give a butterfly with a sore throat?

Antiseptic **moth** wash!

What do you give an ant with a sore throat?

Anti-septic!

TWO TREES

Write down the names of two different trees in the first and last columns of the square to spell five words reading across.

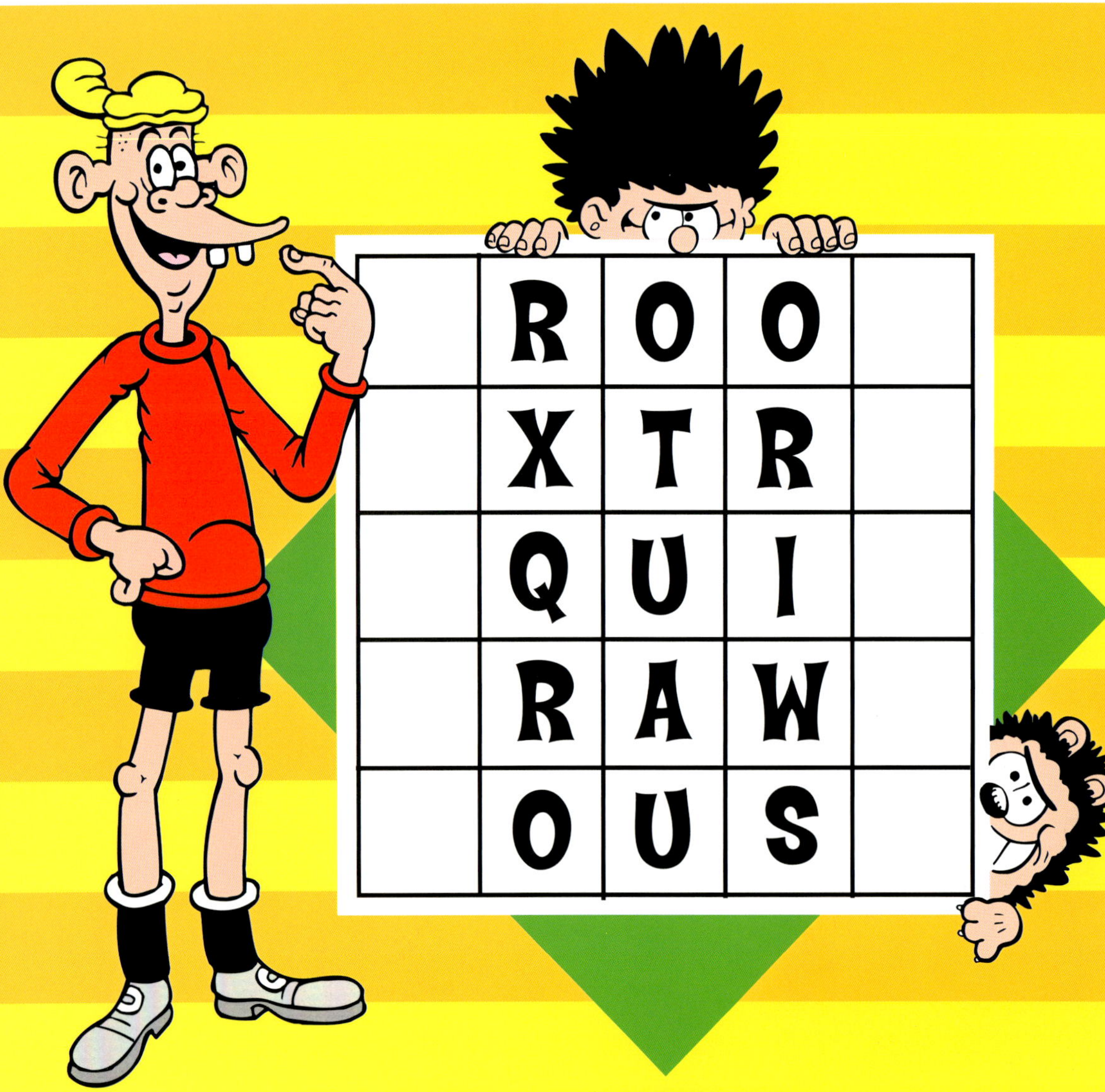

	R	O	O	
	X	T	R	
	Q	U	I	
	R	A	W	
	O	U	S	

NSWER: Beech and Maple

TWOS AND TWOS

There are eight twos on the circles below. Can you write them down in such a way that they will add up to 250?

ANSWER: 222+22+2+2+2=250

What do you call a broken boomerang?

A stick!

What's brown and sticky?

A stick!

What looks like a stick, smells like a stick but isn't a stick?

A stick.

I lied about the last bit!

What is grey, has big ears and a trunk?
A mouse on holiday!

What do you call an arctic cow?

An eskimoo!

Who grants fish three wishes?

The Fairy Codmother!

What fish can fix pianos?

A Tuna fish!

KNOCK! KNOCK!

Who's there?

Aitch.

Aitch who?

I'll come back when your cold is better!

KNOCK! KNOCK!

Who's there?

Tiss.

Tiss who?

Still got a cold then?

SPOT THE DIFFERENCE

Can you spot the five differences between these two pictures of Softy Walter?

ANSWERS: Egg, Worm tail, Tongue, Finger, Lettuce leaf.

REARRANGE THE JUMBLE

Rearrange the jumbled-up letters to spell the names of six countries. The initial letters will then spell another country.

1. LEIGH
2. STAIRUA
3. WEN DALZENA
4. RAMECIA
5. KENMADR
6. ATUASLAIR

ANSWERS: 1. Chile, 2. Austria, 3. New Zealand, 4. America, 5. Denmark, 6. Australia. The initial letters spell 'Canada.'

Why do birds fly south in the winter?

BECAUSE THEY CAN'T AFFORD THE BUS FARE!

What's big and red and stands in the corner?

A naughty bus!

What do you call a girl with a tennis ball on her head?

An-nette!

What do you call a girl with one leg shorter than the other?

Ei-leen!

FALLING OFF A LOG

This puzzle is as easy as falling off a dog – er – log! Just find the names of the dogs that rhyme with the six words on the log.

ANSWER: 1. Collie, 2. Peke, 3. Terrier, 4. Setter, 5. Poodle, 6. Hound, 7. Beagle

ROGER the DODGER
DODGES VOL 1.
DODGES VOL. 4
DODGES VOL. 5
DODGES VOL. 2
DODGES VOL 3
CRISPS
DODGES

What's the difference between snot and sprouts?

Kids won't eat sprouts!

What sits in a bowl of custard looking cross?

Apple Grumble!

NIP, RRIP AND LIP HAVE GONE FISHING — BUT WHICH OF THE LUCKY KITS HAS ACTUALLY CAUGHT A FISH?

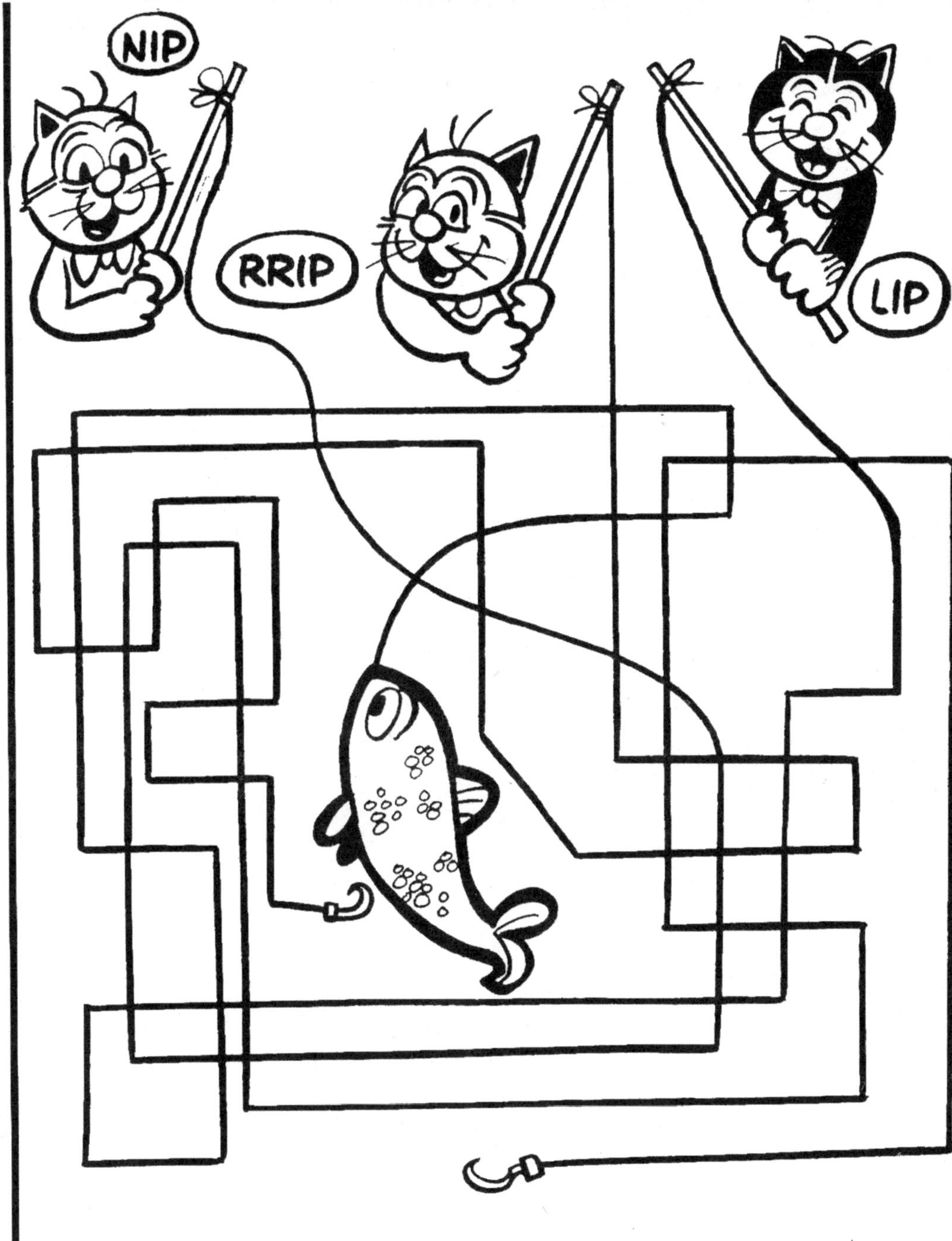

ANSWER Lip.

HERE'S ONE SMIFFY COULDN'T WORK OUT. SEE IF YOU CAN SOLVE IT. BY USING ONLY THE GIVEN LETTERS, SPELL 1. A THREE-LETTER TREE. 2. A FOUR-LETTER SHELLFISH. 3. A FOUR-LETTER MAMMAL. 4. A FIVE-LETTER ANIMAL.
ACE
MLS
ANSWER
1. Elm. 2. Clam. 3. Seal. 4. Camel.

CAN YOU WRITE DOWN THE NAMES OF SIX COUNTRIES WHICH RHYME WITH THE GIVEN GIRLS' NAMES?

1. JANE FROM
2. DINAH FROM
3. ANNE FROM
4. MILLIE FROM
5. DENISE FROM
6. OLIVIA FROM

ANSWER

1. Spain. 2. China. 3. Japan. 4. Chile.
5. Greece. 6. Bolivia.

6
6

HERE'S A CROSSWORD FROM BILLY WHIZZ. SEE HOW QUICKLY YOU CAN SOLVE IT.

ACROSS —
1. A COLOUR.
5. GLUE.
6. NOT WELL.

DOWN —
2. STAND FOR HOLDING ARTIST'S WORK.
3. MONKEY.
4. MARRY.

ANSWER

Across — 1. Red. 5. Paste. 6. Ill.
Down — 2. Easel. 3. Ape. 4. Wed.

KORKY WANTS YOU TO CHANGE ONE LETTER IN THE NAMES OF EACH OF THESE PICTURES TO SPELL 5 ANIMALS.

ANSWER

1. Goat. 2. Bull. 3. Mouse. 4. Ram. 5. Cat.

TEACHER WANTS THE BASH STREET KIDS TO WRITE THE GIVEN NUMBERS, ONE IN EACH BOX, TO MAKE EACH OF THE THREE ROWS ADD TO 51. SEE IF YOU CAN BEAT THEM TO IT.

ANSWER

One answer is A — 12, 18, 21. B — 14, 17, 20. C — 13, 16, 22.

COPY THIS PICTURE OF KORKY THE CAT BY MAKING YOUR LINES CUT THROUGH THE BOXES IN EXACTLY THE SAME PLACES.

1
2
3
4
5
6
7
8
9
10
11
12
13
14
15
16
17
18
19
20
21
22
23
24
25
26
27
28
29
30
31
32
33
34
35
36
37
38
39
40
41
42
43
44
45
46
47
48
49
50
51
52
53
54
55
56
57
58
59
60
61
62
63
64
65
66
67
68
69
70
71
72
73
74
75
76
77
78
79
80
81
82
83
84
85
86
87
88
89
90
91
92
93
94
95
96
97
98
99
100
101
102
103
104
105
106

SEE IF YOU CAN HELP SMIFFY PRINT THE GIVEN NUMBERS IN THE CIRCLES TO MAKE EACH OF THE ROWS TOTAL 30.

ANSWER

1st row — 14, 4, 12.
Bottom row — 8, 16, 6.
Middle row — 10.

DINAH MO'S MUM IS IN THE BUTCHER'S SHOP BUT SHE CAN'T DECIDE WHAT TO BUY FOR TEA. UNSCRAMBLE THE LETTERS TO FIND OUT HER CHOICE.

ANSWER Sausages, roast, pork, chops, bacon, sirloin.

IF YOU PRINT THE CORRECT ANSWERS IN THE BOXES READING ACROSS, THE SAME WORDS WILL READ DOWNWARDS.

1. **MOTOR-ASSISTED BICYCLE.**
2. **MUSICAL DRAMA.**
3. **PART OF A FLOWER.**
4. **RUB OUT.**
5. **VALLEYS.**

ANSWER Moped, opera, petal, erase, dales.

TWO OR MORE CAN PLAY THIS GAME. EACH PLAYER TAKES 10 TURNS DROPPING A PENNY ON THE GNASHERS FROM ABOUT A FOOT ABOVE THE PAPER. THE WINNER IS THE PLAYER WHO COLLECTS THE GREATEST NUMBER OF POINTS INDICATED ON THEIR BACKS. ADD TOGETHER THE POINTS OF EACH GNASHER THE PENNY TOUCHES TO GET YOUR TOTAL SCORES.

7−3
= 2 ✗ 4
8 + 6 =
dunno
we don't
luv
TEECH
2 + 2 = 4
5
9 × 9 = 81
too hard
WATER
WASTE
PAPER
HISTORY

ZZZZ

CAN YOU HELP SOPPY SUSAN FILL IN THE NAMES OF 4 FLOWERS READING INWARDS TOWARDS THE CENTRE? THE 'Y' FORMS THE LAST LETTER OF EACH FLOWER.

ANSWER

Pansy, peony, poppy, daisy.

WHO'D BE A PARENT — ESPECIALLY IF YOU'RE MINNIE'S DAD! USING ONLY THE LETTERS IN "PARENT", TRY TO FIND FIVE WORDS THAT FIT THESE DEFINITIONS — 1. A VEGETABLE. 2. SHORT SLEEP. 3.AN ANIMAL. 4. AN INSECT. 5. A DRINK .

ANSWER

1. Pea. 2. Nap. 3. Rat or Ape. 4. Ant. 5. Tea.

RASHER IS DREAMING ABOUT HIS FAVOURITE FOOD — TURNIPS! ONLY TWO OF THE TURNIPS ARE THE SAME — CAN YOU SPOT THEM?

ANSWER

Nos. 1 and 6.

BALLBOY WANTS YOU TO COMPLETE FIVE GAMES PLAYED WITH A BALL BY PRINTING A LETTER OVER EACH DASH. THE 'O'S ARE IN THE CORRECT POSITION.

1 -O--

2 -O----

3 -O-O

4 -O----

5 --O----

ANSWER

1. Golf. 2. Hockey. 3. Polo. 4. Soccer. 5. Croquet.

DESPERATE DAN IS ALWAYS DREAMING ABOUT FOOD! SEE IF YOU CAN CHANGE ONE LETTER IN EACH WORD TO SPELL SIX FOODS.

ANSWER

1. Pork. 2. Bread. 3. Steak. 4. Bacon. 5. Soup. 6. Lamb.

HERE'S ONE FOR ALL YOU PUZZLERS WHO LIKE A GOOD READ. TEACHER WANTS TO MATCH UP THE BOOKS ON THE LEFT WITH THE CORRECT AUTHORS ON THE RIGHT.

1. TOM SAWYER	A. DANIEL DEFOE
2. OLIVER TWIST	B. JONATHAN SWIFT
3. TREASURE ISLAND	C. SIR WALTER SCOTT
4. GULLIVER'S TRAVELS	D. CHARLES DICKENS
5. ROBINSON CRUSOE	E. MARK TWAIN
6. IVANHOE	F. ROBERT LOUIS STEVENSON

ANSWER

1-E, 2-D, 3-F, 4-B, 5-A, 6-C

1 2 3 4 5 6 7 8 9 10 11 12 13 14 15 16 17 18 19 20 21 22 23 24 25 26 27 28 29 30 31 32 33 34 35 36 37 38 39 40 41 42 43 44 45 46 47 48 49 50 51 52 53 54 55 56 57 58 59 60 61 62 63 64 65 66 67 68 69 70 71 72 73 74 75 76 77 78 79 80 81

YOU'LL FIND THIS JUNIOR CROSSWORD CHILD'S PLAY! JUST FILL IN THE NAMES OF THESE PICTURES IN THE LIKE NUMBERED BOXES READING ACROSS AND DOWN.

ANSWER

Across — 1. Cap. 3. Ant. 5. Oar. 6. Nut. 7. Mop.

Down — 1. Can. 2. Pot. 3. Arm. 4. Top.

DINAH MO HAS BEEN REALLY CLEVER AND DRAWN THIS SQUIRREL USING 17 SINGLE NUMBERS. SEE IF YOU CAN DO IT TOO, THEN ADD UP ALL THE NUMBERS TO SEE HOW MANY ACORNS IT WOULD LIKE!

ANSWER

78 acorns.

A SIMPLE MAZE

Using a pencil, and starting at the bottom right-hand corner, see if you can find your way out of this puzzle.

How many words of three letters or more can you make from the letters on Wilfrid's jersey?

ANSWER —

We found thirty — Ape, apt, ate, east, eats, best, past, paste, pat, pates, pea, peas, peat, peats, pest, sap, sat, sate, sea, spa, spat, spate, step, tap, tape, tapes, tea, teas, ate, pets.

PRINT THE CORRECT LETTERS OVER EACH DASH TO COMPLETE THE NAMES OF SIX TREES, ALL OF WHICH HAVE THE LETTERS 'CH' IN THEIR NAMES.

ANSWER

1. Cherry. 2. Larch. 3. Peach. 4. Birch. 5. Beech. 6. Chestnut.

FRUIT & VEG
GNASH GNASH GNASH!
ZOOM

TEACHER
TEACHER
TEACHER
TEACHER
SPLAT!
SLIP!

THIS ONE'S GOT SMIFFY STUMPED – SEE IF YOU CAN DO IT! WRITE THE NUMBERS FROM 1-13 IN THE BOXES TO MAKE THEM TOTAL THE EXACT AMOUNT AT THE END OF THE 11 ROWS INDICATED BY THE ARROWS. YOU CAN ONLY USE THE NUMBERS ONCE!

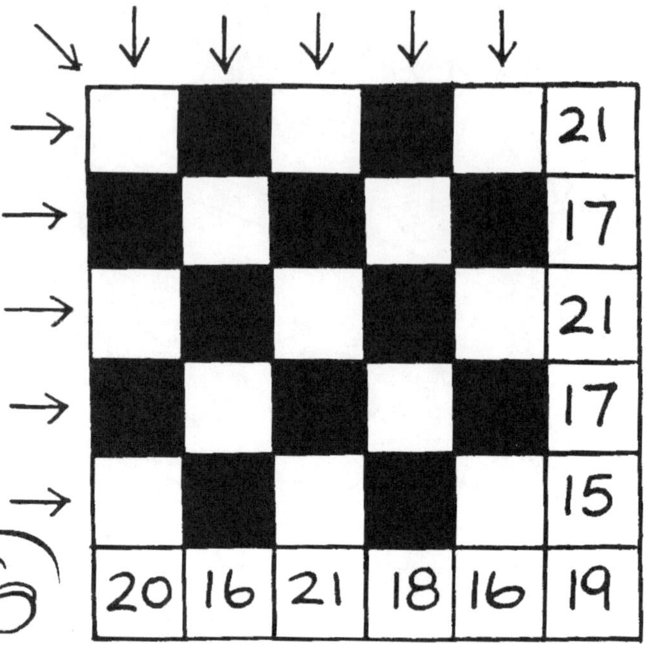

ANSWER —

Across from the top — 7, 8, 6; 4, 13; 10, 2, 9; 12, 5; 3, 11, 1.

KARATE SID IS CHOPPING UP WOOD AND IT WON'T TAKE HIM LONG BY THE LOOK OF IT! CAN YOU TURN 'CHOP' INTO 'WOOD' IN FOUR MOVES, CHANGING ONE LETTER AT A TIME TO FORM A NEW WORD AT EACH STEP?

ANSWER

Chop, coop, cool, wool, wood is one solution.

LORD SNOOTY LIKES HIS SERVICE FROM HIS BUTLER. SEE HOW MANY WORDS OF THREE OR MORE LETTERS YOU CAN MAKE FROM THE LETTERS IN *BUTLER*. USE EACH LETTER ONLY ONCE IN EACH WORD.

BUTLER

ANSWER

But, bet, let, rub, rue, rut, tub, blue, rule, rebut are 10.

OUR ARTIST HAS DRAWN ONLY HALF OF THIS PICTURE OF DINAH MO. SEE IF YOU CAN FINISH IT OFF FOR HIM.

HOW MANY MINUTES IS IT PAST TWO IF THIRTY FIVE MINUTES AGO, IT WAS TWICE AS MANY MINUTES PAST ONE?
I DON'T KNOW, ROGER.
ANSWER
The answer is twenty-five past two.

JUGGLE EACH GROUP OF LETTERS TO SPELL FIVE THINGS DINAH MO GOT FOR HER BIRTHDAY. THEY ARE ALL THINGS YOU CAN WEAR!

ANSWER

Ring, scarf, watch, gloves, bracelet.

1
2
3
4
5
6
7
8
9
10
11
12
13
14
15
16
17
18

OUR ARTIST HAS DONE IT AGAIN. HE'S DRAWN 5 PUZZLE BOOK CHARACTERS WITH CERTAIN BITS MISSING. CAN YOU SPOT WHAT THEY ARE?

ANSWER

Roger's tie, Ivy's hair, Gnasher's ears, Ballboy's hair and Rasher's gnashers!

DRAW FOUR STRAIGHT LINES FROM BORDER TO BORDER TO MAKE EACH LINE PASS THROUGH THREE LOLLIPOPS.

ANSWER

Draw lines through 7, 10, 3; 8, 2, 5; 9, 1, 6; 12, 4, 11.

MA

SEE IF YOU CAN COMPLETE AT LEAST EIGHT GIRLS' NAMES THAT BEGIN WITH THE LETTERS 'MA'.

1. MA
2. MA
3. MA
4. MA
5. MA
6. MA
7. MA
8. MA

ANSWER

Mary, Madeline, Mavis, Margaret, Mandy, Marilyn, Marlene, Marie, Maria, Martha, Marjorie, Maureen, Matilda are 13.

N.P.

WALTER IS OUT FOR A WALK WITH FOUR PALS. TO FIND OUT THEIR NAMES, SHADE IN ALL THE BOXES THAT HAVE AN ODD NUMBER.

ANSWER Anthony, Michael, Peter and Stewart.

Here are twelve words. Tick those that you think are spelt correctly, and put crosses against the others. Then check with the solution.

Answer:

Nos. 2, 4, 5, 7, 9, 10 and 11 are spelt correctly. 'Cabbige' should be 'Cabbage', 'Calipso' should be 'Calypso', 'Capcize' should be 'Capsize', 'Chedder' should be 'Cheddar' and 'Concent' should be 'Consent'.

What was the farmer doing on the other side of the road?

Waiting for his chickens!

Why did the fish cross the road?

To get his bicycle!

What is black and white and black and white and black and white?

A penguin rolling down a hill!

What is black and white and red at the top?

A sunburnt penguin!

What is black and white and red at the bottom?

A sunburnt penguin standing on its head!

What has four legs and goes oom oom?

A cow walking backwards!

What has four legs and goes oow oow?

A cow in Australia!

SPOT THE DIFFERENCE

Can you spot five differences between these two pictures of Dennis and Gnasher?

SWERS: Kettle, Comic, Cereal packet, Milk jug,
sher's teeth.

What's the difference between a **cat** and a **frog**?

A cat has **nine** lives, but a frog croaks **every night!**

What did the frog order at the fast food restaurant?

*French **flies** and a diet **croak**!*

Dennis: Do you want to hear the joke about the rare disease?

Walter: Yes please!

Dennis: What's the point - you'll never get it!

Dennis: Do you want to hear the joke about the dustbin?

Walter: Is it good?

Dennis: No - it's

Rubbish!

SPOT THE DIFFERENCE

Can you spot five differences between these two pictures of Ivy?

NSWERS: Tooth, Shoe, Pocket, Ear, Hair.

10 LETTERS ★ 10 ANIMALS

Use the ten letters as often as you like to try to spell at least ten animals.

A B D E

G L O R

S T

ANSWERS: Here are ten: Badger, Bear, Boar, Deer, Doe, Dog, Goat, Rat, Seal and Stag

Why shouldn't you eat green elephants?

Because they're not ripe yet!

What is grey and squirts jam at you?

An elephant eating a doughnut!

HOW DO SPACEMEN TIE THEIR SHOELACES?

WITH ASTRO-KNOTS!

How do fish tie their shoelaces?

They don't have shoelaces - they only have soles!

HOW DOES ROBIN HOOD TIE HIS SHOELACES?

WITH A BOW!

SPOT THE DIFFERENCE

Can you spot five differences between these two pictures of Dennis?

ANSWERS: Pop label, Dagger, Fingers, Earring, Sock.

IN THE KITCHEN

Place a letter in each blank to make the letters spell seven things found in the kitchen. The clues are on the left.

1. An implement to eat with. _ _ _ K
2. You wash dishes in it. _ _ _ I _
3. Used for cooking. _ _ T
4. You drink from it. C _ _
5. A plate. _ _ _ H
6. A container for boiling water. _ E _ _ _ _
7. Used for cutting. _ N _ _ _

ANSWERS: 1. Fork, 2. Basin, 3. Pot, 4. Cup, 5. Dish, 6. Kettle, 7. Knife

Dennis: **Doctor! Doctor! I think I've turned into Gnasher!**

Doctor: **Sit down and tell me all about it.**

Dennis: **I can't - I'm not allowed on the furniture!**

What do giraffes have that other animals don't have?

Baby giraffes!

Why don't grasshoppers play football?

They prefer **cricket**!

ANIMAL TABLE

Can you complete the table, using only the words around Dennis? The numbers in the brackets tell you how many to look for.

LIZARDS

MOSQUITOES

MICE

SWANS

SNAKES

RABBITS

EAGLES

OWLS

GIRAFFES

BEETLES

TORTOISES

WASPS

1. Insects (3) ------------------------
2. Birds (3) ------------------------
3. Reptiles (3) ------------------------
4. Rodents (2) ------------------------
5. Stingers (3) ------------------------
6. Long Necks (2) ------------------------
7. Mammals (3) ------------------------
8. Have long tails (3) ------------------------
9. The largest (1) ------------------------
10. The smallest (1) ------------------------

ANSWER: 1. Mosquitoes, Beetles, Wasps; 2. Swans, Eagles, Owls; 3. Lizards, Snakes, Tortoises; 4. Mice, Rabbits; 5. Mosquitoes, Snakes, Wasps; 6. Swans, Giraffes; 7. Mice, Rabbits, Giraffes; 8. Mice, Lizards, Giraffes; 9. Giraffes; 10. Mosquitoes

COUNTRY MATCH

Which country do you associate the following?

1. KANGAROO
2. MOUNTIES
3. JOHN BULL
4. THE RISING SUN
5. SHAMROCK
6. UNCLE SAM
7. KILTS
8. SOMBRERO
9. SPAGHETTI
10. SNAILS
11. CORK
12. SARIS

CHOOSE THE COUNTRIES FROM THIS LIST:

IRELAND
SCOTLAND
PORTUGAL
CANADA
INDIA
AUSTRALIA
ITALY
MEXICO
FRANCE
JAPAN
USA
BRITAIN

1. Australia, 2. Canada, 3. Britain, 4. Japan, 5. Ireland, 6. USA, 7. Scotland, 8. Mexico, 9. Italy, 10. France, 11. Portugal, 12. India

What do you call a boy with a plank on his head?

Ed-wood!

What do you call a boy with a seagull on his head?

Cliff!

KNOCK! KNOCK!

Who's there?

The engineer.

The engineer who?

The engineer who came to fix your doorbell!

KNOCK! KNOCK!

Who's there?

The engineer again.

The engineer again who?

The engineer again who couldn't fix your doorbell, but the door seems to be working!

SPOT THE DIFFERENCE

Can you spot five differences in these two pictures of Desperate Dan?

SWERS: Comic, Spur, Neckerchief, Arm, Chair Arm.

MISSING WORDS

The missing words in the centre have the same meaning as the words on either side. Try to work them out.

1. RUBBISH		CHINESE BOAT
2. PEAK		SPINNING TOY
3. CUT DOWN		A HILL
4. RHYTHM		DEFEAT
5. DISTRIBUTE CARDS		A LOT
6. SUPPORTER		KEEPS YOU COOL

ANSWERS: 1. Junk, 2. Top, 3. Fell, 4. Beat, 5. Deal, 6. Fan

Dennis: Dad! I think this violin is broken!

Dad: Well stop blowing it then!

Dennis: Dad! I think my alarm clock is made of cheese!

Dad: Why's that?

Dennis: It keeps going off!

Did you hear the one about the ship full of yo-yos that hit a rock?

It sunk 37 times!

How many rude people does it take to change a light bulb?

None of your business!!!

SPOT THE DIFFERENCE

Can you spot five differences between these two pictures of Dennis and Gnasher?

ANSWERS: Fingers, Egg in box, Stripe on jersey, Box, Tail.

STARTLING

Drop one letter from the word 'STARTLING' and make an eight-letter word. Keep doing this until you reach a one-letter word.

9. Startling

8. ---------

7. --------

6. ------

5. -----

4. ----

3. ---

2. --

1. -

ANSWERS: Startling, Starting, Staring, String, Sting, Sing, Sin, In, I

What goes 99-thump, 99-thump, 99-thump?

A centipede with a wooden leg!

What goes 99-thump-clunk-clunk, 99-thump-clunk-clunk, 99-thump-clunk-clunk?

A centipede with a wooden leg and crutches!

What goes tring! tring! whizz?

A centipede with a wooden leg riding a bicycle!

What's pink and wobbles?

A jellybaby!

What's the difference between babies and football players?

One drools and the other dribbles!

SPOT THE DIFFERENCE

Can you spot five differences betweeen these two pictures of Smiffy?

ANSWERS: Saddle, Chain, Pedal , Cuff, Sock.

DENNIS the MENACE

What's green and hangs from trees?

Monkey snot!

What's green and hangs from caves?

A sick bat!

What's the slowest animal on earth?

A snail with a limp!

What's the fastest animal on earth?

A snail with a rocket strapped to its back!

Why shouldn't you take a crocodile to the zoo?

Because they'd rather go to the cinema!

What is hairy and coughs?

A sick coconut!

BY USING ONLY THE LETTERS IN 'TELEVISION', TRY TO HELP RASHER SPELL 6 FIVE-LETTER WORDS TO FIT THE FOLLOWING DEFINITIONS —

Television

1. SOUND.
2. NUMBER.
3. THEY COUNT IN AN ELECTION.
4. A STRONG METAL.
5. 14 LB.
6. APPARATUS FOR COOKING.

Answer

1. Noise. 2. Seven. 3. Votes. 4. Steel. 5. Stone. 6. Stove.

IVY THE TERRIBLE'S DAD IS TRYING TO HAVE A DOZE IN THE CHAIR — BUT IVY PREFERS HIM AWAKE! CAN YOU CHANGE 'DOZE' to 'WAKE' IN 4 MOVES, ALTERING ONE LETTER TO FORM A NEW WORD AT EACH MOVE?

ANSWER — Doze, daze, laze, lake, wake is one solution.

USE UP ALL THE GIVEN LETTERS TO SPELL THREE WORDS MEANING 'SMALL'.

ANSWER

Little, tiny, minute.

MOVE FROM LETTER TO LETTER IN ANY DIRECTION TO SPELL AT LEAST SEVEN THINGS THE BASH STREET KIDS MIGHT USE IN THE CLASSROOM.

R	A	Y	L	U
I	C	O	E	R
L	O	N	B	P
R	I	K	S	A
E	D	E	P	D
S	A	R	X	S

ANSWER

Ruler, desk, pen, pencil, crayon, ink, book, eraser are eight.

wiLfrid
Teacher
sPotTy
DanNy
toots
siDney
fatty
Plug
CuthBert
'Erbert
SMiffY

SEE IF YOU CAN COPY THE GRID DRAWING OF JONAH IN THE SIMILAR EMPTY GRID BELOW.

IVY THE TERRIBLE'S DAD IS LOOKING THROUGH SOME BROCHURES FOR SOMEWHERE TO GO ON HOLIDAY. REARRANGE EACH SET OF LETTERS TO FIND OUT THE NAMES OF SIX DIFFERENT COUNTRIES, AND THE INITIAL LETTERS WILL THEN SPELL ANOTHER COUNTRY.

ANSWER

Finland, Russia, Argentina, Norway, Canada and Ecuador. The initial letters spell France.

TAKE THE INITIALS OF THE SEVEN DRAWINGS SHOWN AND REARRANGE THEM TO SPELL THE NAME OF A MONTH.

Answer

January.

BALLBOY WANTS YOU TO REARRANGE THE JUMBLED UP LETTERS TO SPELL THE NAME OF 5 BRITISH FOOTBALL GROUNDS. THEN SEE IF YOU KNOW WHICH TEAM PLAYS THERE!

ANSWER

Upton Park (West Ham United), Easter Road (Hibs), Anfield (Liverpool), Turf Moor (Burnley), The Dell (Southampton).

SEE IF YOU CAN COMPLETE FIVE WORDS ON THE RIGHT FROM THE CLUES ON THE LEFT. ALL WORDS END IN 'EEK'.

ANSWER

Greek, week, leek, seek, sleek.

TANGLED LETTERS

Can you make out how many letters of the alphabet are mixed up in this puzzle?

Q, F, J, E, B, W, D

HARD PEAS
MID-MORNING SNACK
HOMEWORK
WASTE PAPER

⅓ OF BAY, ⅖ OF OCEAN, ¼ OF CRAB, AND ⅕ OF SHORE WILL SPELL WHAT POPULAR AREA BESIDE THE WATER?

ANSWER

Beach.

THE BADD LADS HID THEIR LOOT, BUT THEY CAN'T REMEMBER WHERE! SEE IF YOU CAN HELP THEM BY CHANGING *LOSE* TO *FIND* IN 4 STEPS, ALTERING ONE LETTER TO FORM ANOTHER WORD AT EACH MOVE.

LOSE

___

___

___

FIND

ANSWER

Lose, lone, line, fine is one solution.

HERE'S A GEOGRAPHY LESSON FROM TEACHER. READING ACROSS, PRINT A LETTER IN EACH BLANK SQUARE TO SPELL THE NAMES OF 9 COUNTRIES. THE WORD 'GEOGRAPHY' HAS BEEN WRITTEN IN TO HELP YOU.

ANSWER

Reading across from the top — Hungary, Sweden, Norway, England, Germany, Canada, Japan, China, Egypt.

1
2
3
4
5
6
7
8
9
10
11
12
13
14
15
16
17
18
19
20
21
22
23
24
25
26
27
28
29
30
31
32
33
34
35
36
37
38
39
40
41
42
43
44

BALLBOY HAS THOUGHT UP THESE FUNNY DRAWINGS, ALL CONNECTED WITH FOOTBALL. SEE IF YOU CAN WORK OUT WHAT THEY ARE.

ANSWER

1. A 'fowl' tackle. 2. Injury time. 3. A key player. 4. A diving header.

SEE IF YOU CAN HELP SOPPY SUSAN CHANGE *ROSE* TO *PINK* IN FOUR STEPS.

ROSE

____

____

____

PINK

ANSWER

Rose, rise, risk, rink, pink is one solution.

AFTER ROGER THE DODGER FOUND £2 IN THE STREET, HE THEN HAD THREE TIMES AS MUCH AS HE WOULD HAVE HAD IF HE HAD LOST £2. HOW MUCH DID HE HAVE BEFORE HE FOUND THE £2?

ANSWER

Roger had £4 before he found the £2.

JONAH WANTS YOU TO DRAW ONE STRAIGHT LINE TO COMPLETE EACH LETTER TO SPELL 4 FOUR-LETTER PARTS OF A SHIP.

ANSWER:

1. Mast. 2. Keel. 3. Deck. 4. Hull.

THIS CROSS-NUMBER PUZZLE HAS GOT SMIFFY CROSS-EYED. SEE IF YOU CAN SOLVE IT. WRITE THE NUMBERS FROM 1-12 IN EACH EMPTY BOX SO THAT EACH OF THE 8 ROWS INDICATED WILL TOTAL THE AMOUNT SHOWN AT THE END OF THE ROW.

ANSWER

1st row across — 1, 12, 6.
2nd row across — 11, 2, 9.
3rd row across — 5, 8, 7.
4th row across — 4, 10, 3.

REARRANGE THE GROUPS OF LETTERS ON BIFFO'S CASE TO FIND OUT WHICH COUNTRIES HE IS GOING TO VISIT ON HIS HOLIDAYS.
STATION
FCA ENR
YE P GT
YAL IT
UIB ELGM
PA IS N
ANSWER France, Italy, Belgium, Spain, Egypt.

THIS REALLY GOT SMIFFY'S HUMP! TEACHER MADE HIM DRAW A CAMEL ON THE BLACKBOARD USING SINGLE NUMBERS— NOW HE WANTS HIM TO ADD THEM ALL UP! SEE IF YOU CAN HELP HIM GET THE ANSWER.
ANSWER The total is 110.

SOFTY WALTER WANTS YOU TO FIND THE ANSWERS TO THE GIVEN CLUES, THEN PRINT THEM, ONE LETTER OVER EACH DASH, TO SPELL THE NAMES OF SIX OF HIS PALS.

ANSWER 1. Richard. 2. Roland. 3. Stanley. 4. Lionel. 5. Patrick. 6. Timothy.

4 DOZ. ROTTEN EGGS

ARRANGE THE NUMBERS 3 - 9 IN THE BLANK SPACES, SO THAT EACH ROW ADDS UP TO 20

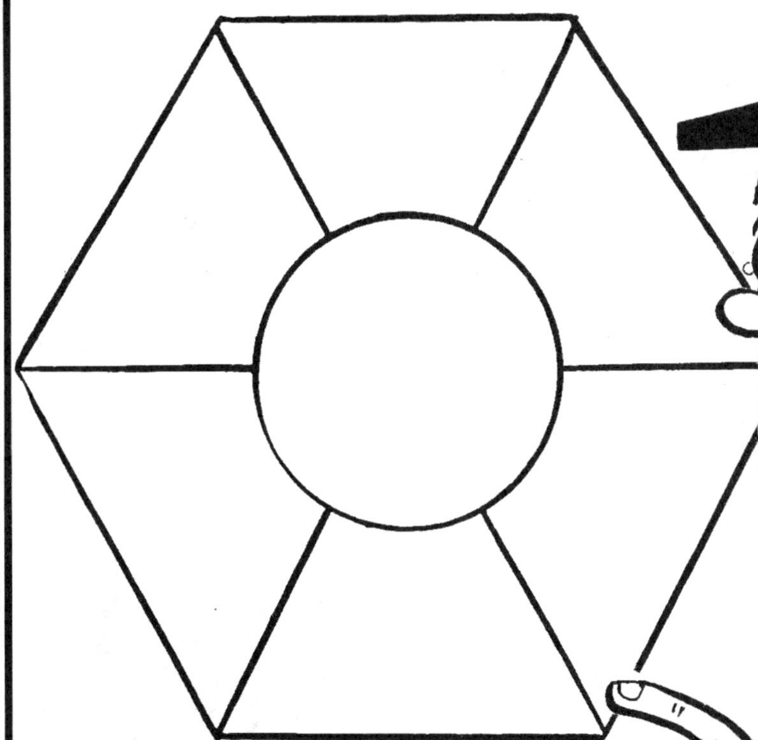

ANSWER

Clockwise from the top — 6, 4, 8, 5, 7, 3, with 9 in the middle.

YOU CAN COPY THIS PICTURE OF TEACHER IN THE EMPTY GRID BY MAKING YOUR LINES CUT THROUGH THE BOXES IN EXACTLY THE SAME POSITIONS AS THEY DO IN THE ORIGINALS.

THESE PARCELS ARRIVED FOR THE BASH STREET KIDS BUT THE NAMES ON THE LABELS ARE JUMBLED UP. REARRANGE THE LETTERS TO FIND OUT WHO GETS EACH PARCEL.

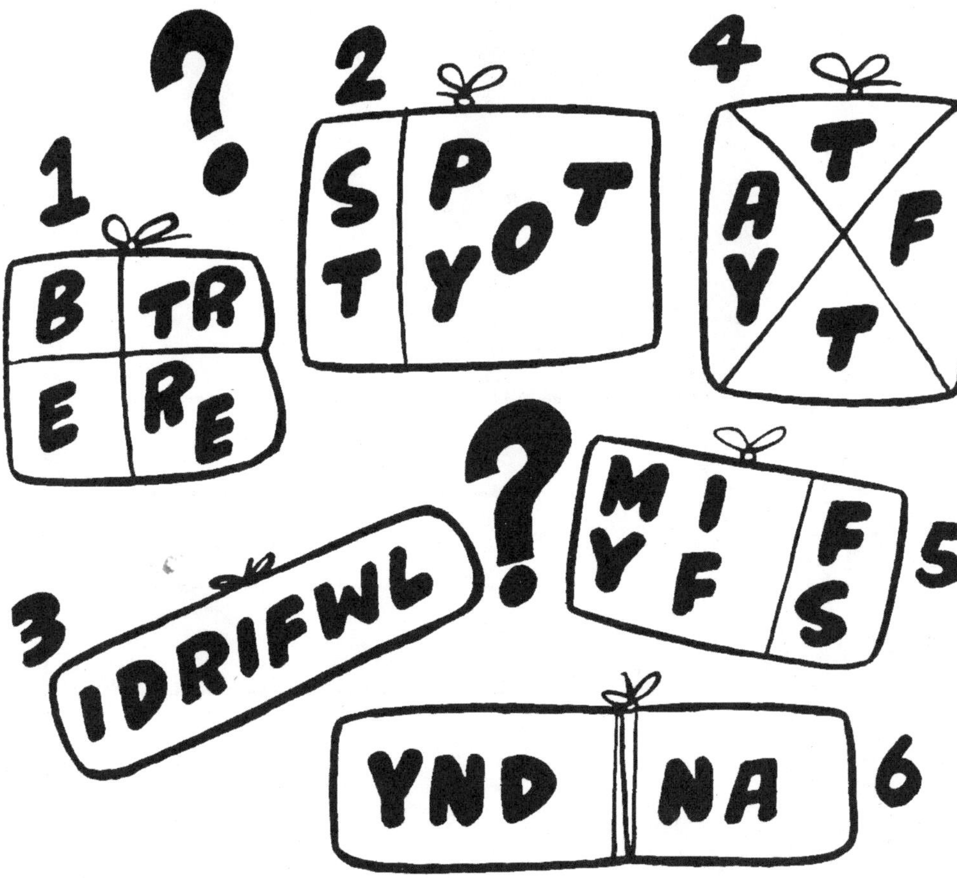

ANSWER

1. 'Erbert. 2. Spotty. 3. Wilfrid. 4. Fatty. 5. Smiffy. 6. Danny.

A YOUNG BEAR, AS YOU KNOW, IS A CUB (BIFFO WAS ONE ONCE!) BUT DO YOU KNOW WHAT THE YOUNG OF THE SIX LISTED CREATURES ARE CALLED?

ANSWER

Gosling, squab, calf, kid, fawn, pup.

WHAT THREE NUMBERS WILL LITTLE PLUM HAVE TO HIT SO THAT HIS TOTAL SCORE WILL BE 80?

ANSWER 17 + 39 + 24 = 80

DESERT ISLAND DICK WANTS YOU TO TRY TO SAY THIS TRICKY TONGUE TWISTER AS QUICKLY AS POSSIBLE —

HOW DID THE FLY ESCAPE?

Some of the threads were broken and so the fly got away safely. Can you see which way he went?

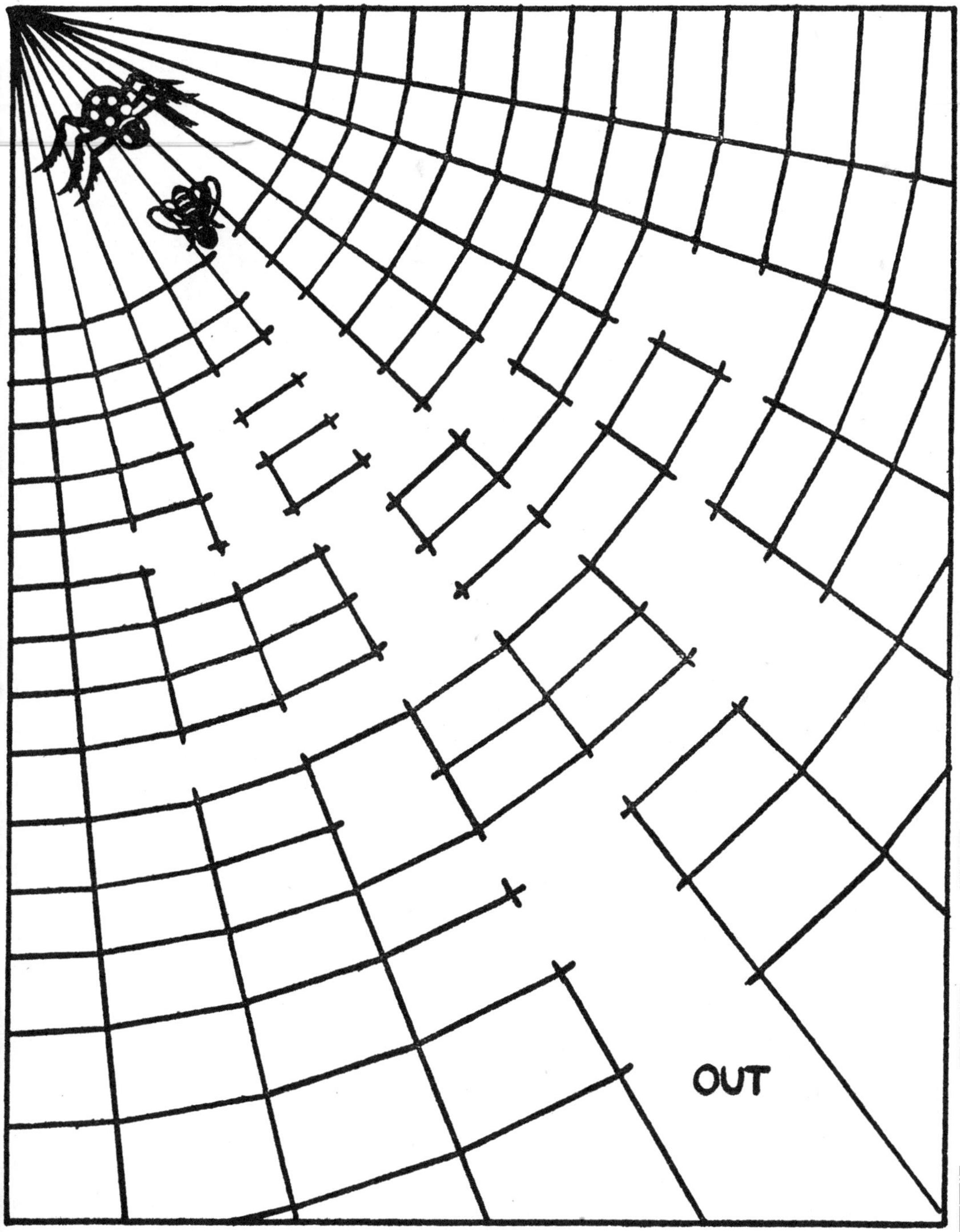

SEE IF YOU CAN CHANGE *PUP* TO *DOG* IN FOUR MOVES, CHANGING ONE LETTER AT A TIME TO FORM A NEW WORD AT EACH STEP.

ANSWER

Pup, pip, dip, dig, dog is one solution.

ANSWER

14 pigs and 22 hens.

RASHER WANTS YOU TO SEE IF YOU CAN NAME THESE BRITISH CITIES FROM THE PICTURE CLUES.

1

2

3

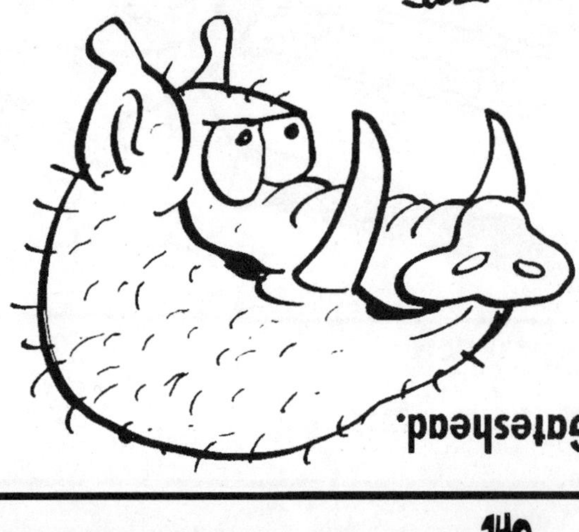

ANSWER

Manchester, Glasgow and Gateshead.

USE UP ALL THE GIVEN LETTERS TO HELP SOPPY SUSAN SPELL TWO WORDS THAT SOUND THE SAME BUT HAVE DIFFERENT MEANINGS.

WFOORLEURFL

ANSWER

Flower and flour.

DINAH MO'S MUM IS MAKING A POT OF SOUP — BUT WHAT KIND IS IT? REARRANGE THE LETTERS ON THE POT TO FIND OUT!
PANDA HAME
ANSWER
Pea and ham.

1
2
3
4
5
6
7
8
9
10
11
12
13
14
15
16
17
18
19
20
21
22
23
24
25
26
27
28
29
30
31
32
33
34
35
36
37
38
39
40
41
42
43
44
45
46
47
48
49
50
51
52
53
54
55
56
57
58
59

SPOT THE PAIR

Only two of these really match. Can you see which make a pair?

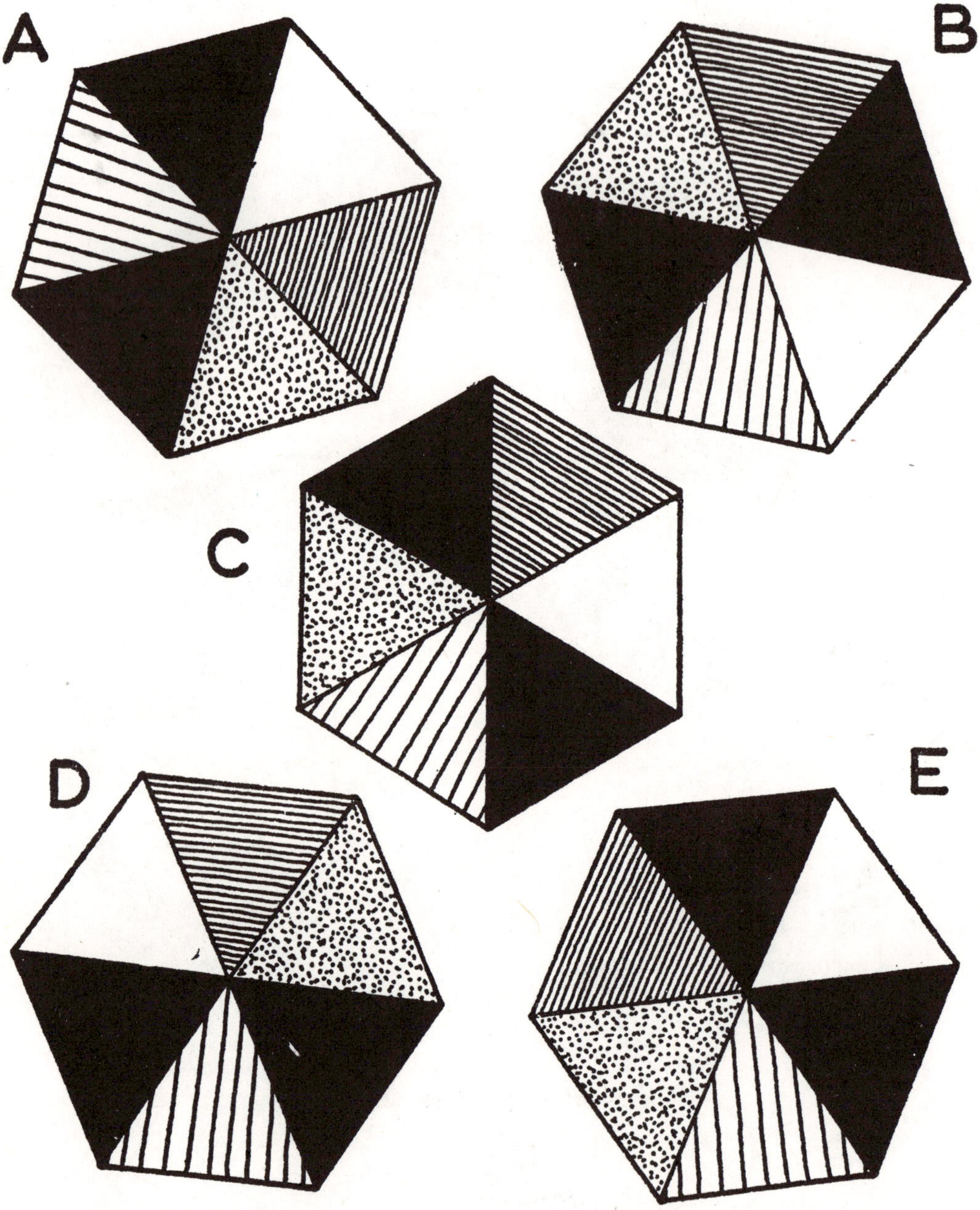

A and D

What do you get if you put Walter's favourite toy in the freezer?

A teddy-brrrrrr!

What do you get if you run over Walter's favourite toy with a lawnmower?

A shreddy-bear!

What do you call a girl with a church on her head?

ABBY!

What do you call a girl with a draughty church on her head?

ABI-GALE!

What's small, brown and fluffy?

A toffee that's been in your pocket for weeks!

What's brown, yellow and hairy?

Cheese on toast that fell on the carpet!

Can you match the words below with each riddle?

A BED

AN UMBRELLA

A COMB

DRAUGHTS

AN ANGLE

A PHOTOGRAPH

A NOISE

1. What can you make that no one can see? ______
2. What can't you have for dinner or tea? ______
3. What has four legs, but only one foot? ______
4. What is best when it's used up? ______
5. What can be right but not wrong? ______
6. What do you go out for but never bring back? ______
7. What are the best things to put into a currant bin? ______
8. What do you get after it's been taken? ______
9. What is the best thing to give as a parting gift? ______
10. What did the North wind play? ______

A WALK

BREAKFAST

TEETH

ANSWERS: 1. A noise, 2. Breakfast, 3. A bed, 4. An umbrella, 5. An angle, 6. A walk, 7. Teeth, 8. A photograph, 9. A comb, 10. Draughts

SPOT THE DIFFERENCE

Can you spot the five differences between these two pictures of Sidney and Smiffy?

ANSWERS: Drumstick, Tongue, Tie, Collar, Knee.

Why did the chicken cross the road?

No one is eggs-actly sure!

Why did the second chicken cross the road?

He did it as a yolk!

What's the best way of counting cows?

With a cow-culator!

What tool can help you with your sums?

Multi-pliers!

GIRLS' NAMES

Change just one letter in each of the eight words below to spell eight girls' names.

1★ JUNK __________

2★ ROAN __________

3★ BOTH __________

4★ LEAN __________

5★ GLEN __________

6★ PANE __________

7★ FATE __________

8★ JILT __________

ANSWERS: 1. June, 2. Joan, 3. Beth, 4. Jean, 5. Gwen, 6. Jane, 7. Kate, 8. Jill

DOGGY SCRAMBLE

Unscramble the groups of letters below to spell out the names of six dogs.

ANSWERS: 1. Bloodhound, 2. Airedale, 3. Spaniel, 4. Terrier, 5. Collie, 6. Poodle.

What do you call a sheep with a parachute?

A woolly jumper!

What do you call a sheep with a parachute that pushes in front of you?

A woolly queue jumper!

What's a pirate's favourite pudding?

Jelly-Roger!

Why do sharks live in saltwater?

Because pepper makes them sneeze!

SPOT THE DIFFERENCE

Can you spot the five differences between these two pictures of Roger the Dodger?

ANSWERS: Hair, Collar, Hand, Knot in fence, Fence top.

SPELLING★

To complete this word game, you have to spell at least eight four-letter words using only the letters in the word 'FRANCE'.

ANSWERS: Face, Fear, Race, Care, Café, Near, Fare and Cane are 8.

What two vegetables do you find in the toilet?

Leeks and peas!

What has a bottom at the top?

Your legs!

What's a mouse's
favourite game?

Hide and squeak!

What is a cat's
favourite breakfast?

Mice crispies!

'N'S

Fill in the names of six Euro countries. The 'N's are in the correct position.

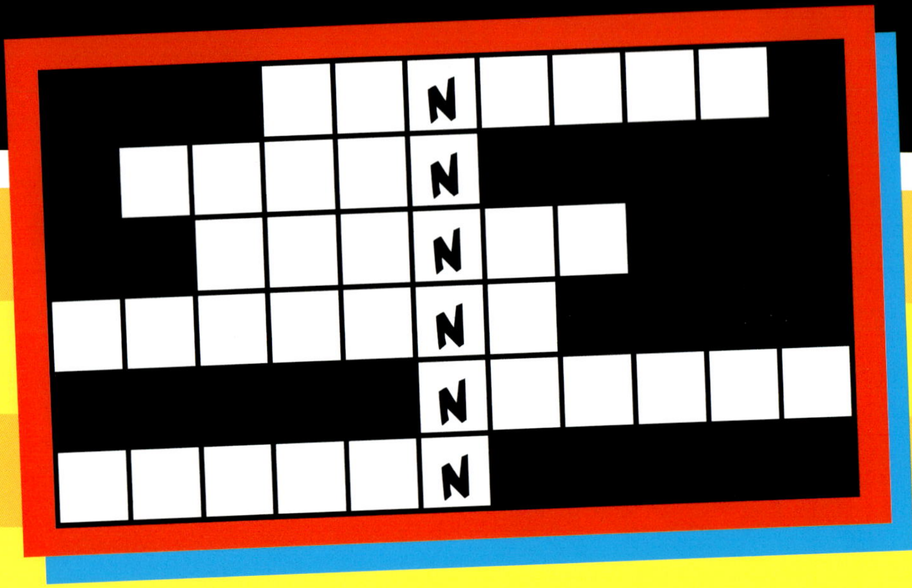

ANSWERS: Finland, Spain, France, Germany, Norway, Sweden

MiNNiE
the MiNX

KNOCK! KNOCK!

Who's there?

Want.

Want who?

Good - now try counting to three!

KNOCK! KNOCK!

Who's there?

Boo.

Boo who?

Don't cry - it's only a joke!

What kind of vegetables do maths teachers eat?

SQUARE ROOTS!

What sort of vegetables do history teachers eat?

HAS-BEANS!

WINDOW SHOPPING

What six types of shops are featured in these shop windows?

ANSWERS: 1. Baker, 2. Newsagent, 3. Cobbler, 4. Chemist, 5. Tailor, 6. Butcher.

SPOT THE DIFFERENCE

Can you spot the five differences between these two pictures of Minnie the Minx?

ANSWERS: Chips, Tail, Pom-pom, Jersey, Wheel.

What do you call a snowman in the desert?

A puddle!

What do you call an eskimo's house with no toilet?

An ig!

What's the best way to catch a fish?

Get someone to throw one at you!

Are dolphins ever naughty by accident?

No - they always do it on porpoise!

DESPERATE DAN

Desperate Dan just loves cow pie. Try to solve the clues to find another five words that start with cow.

1. Faint-hearted person.	C	O	W				
2. Looks after cattle.	C	O	W				
3. A monk's hood.	C	O	W				
4. Crouch in fear.	C	O	W				
5. A flower	C	O	W				

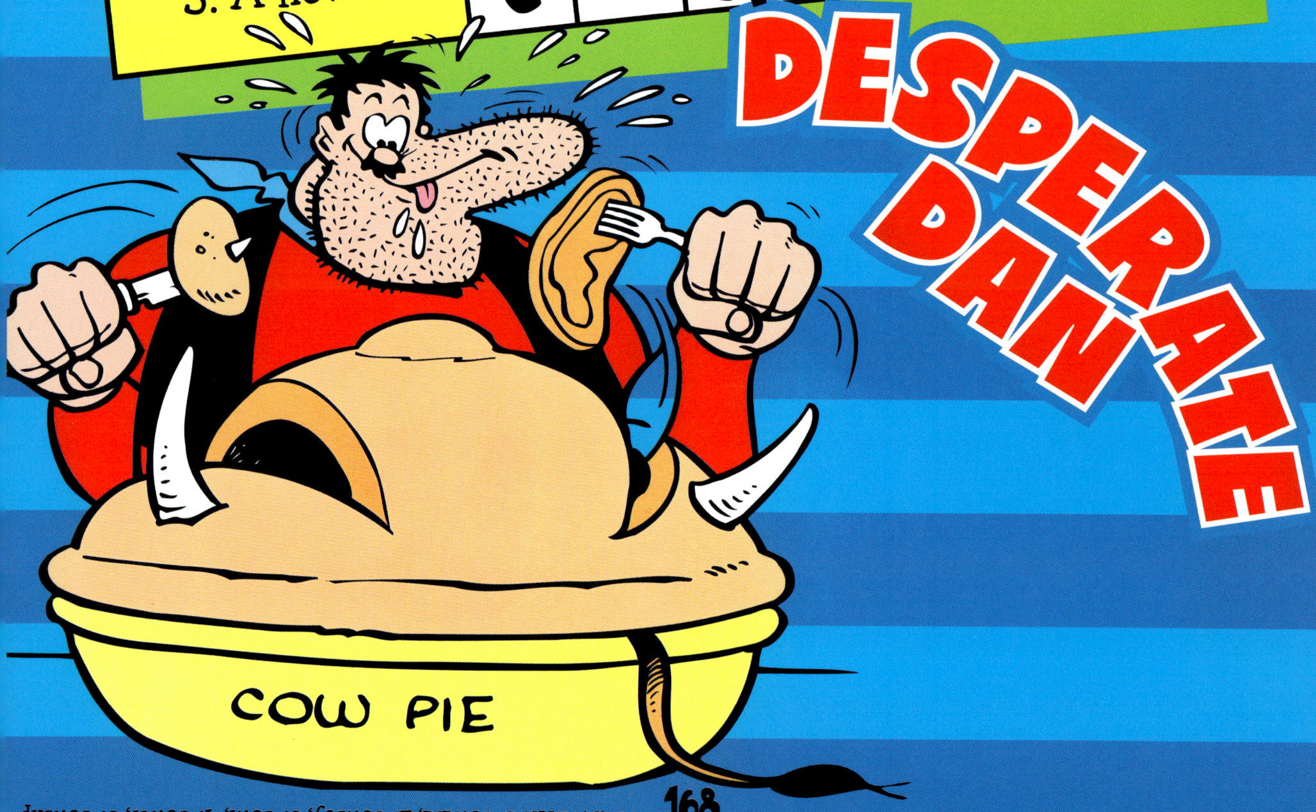

ANSWERS: 1. Coward, 2. Cowboy, 3. Cowl, 4. Cower, 5. Cowslip

HOW MANY?

Teacher wants to see if you know your numbers.

A. Pheasants in a brace?
B. Millimetres in a centimetre?
C. Dancers in a pas de deux?
D. Squares on a draughts board?
E. Legs on a bantam?
F. Years in a decade?
G. Wheels on a tandem?
H. Gospels in the New Testament?
I. Tentacles on an octopus?
J. Strings on a violin?
K. Lines on a musical stave?
L. Dots on a dice?

ANSWERS: A. 2, B. 10, C. 2, D. 64, E. 2, F. 10, G. 2, H. 4, I. 8, J. 4, K. 5, L. 21

Why do ducks
have webbed feet?

So they can kick spiders!

What are
invisible and
smell of carrots?

Rabbit farts!

Why do humming birds hum?

Because they don't know the words!

How do you stop birds building nests?

Take away their tool belts!

FINDING APPLIANCES

Hidden in each of the three sentences below is an electrical appliance found in most homes. Try to spot all three.

1. PLEASE PROVIDE ORANGES AND APPLES.

2. I SAW A FIR - ONCE.

3. THE CLIFF RIDGE IS VERY HIGH.

ANSWERS: 1. Video, 2. Iron, 3. Fridge

WORDMAKER

How many words of three letters or more can you make from the letters below Dennis and Gnasher?

ANSWERS: Here are 30: Ape, Apt, Ate, East, Eats, Best, Past, Paste, Pat, Pates, Pea, Peas, Peat, Peats, Pest, Sap, Sat, Sate, Sea, Spa, Spat, Spate, Step, Tap, Tape, Tapes, Tea, Teas, Ate, Pets

Why did the dinosaur cross the road?

Because chickens hadn't been invented yet!

Where do dinosaurs wear ties?

Around their tyrannosaurus necks!

Walter: How many eggs does it take to make a stink bomb?

Dennis: Quite a phew!

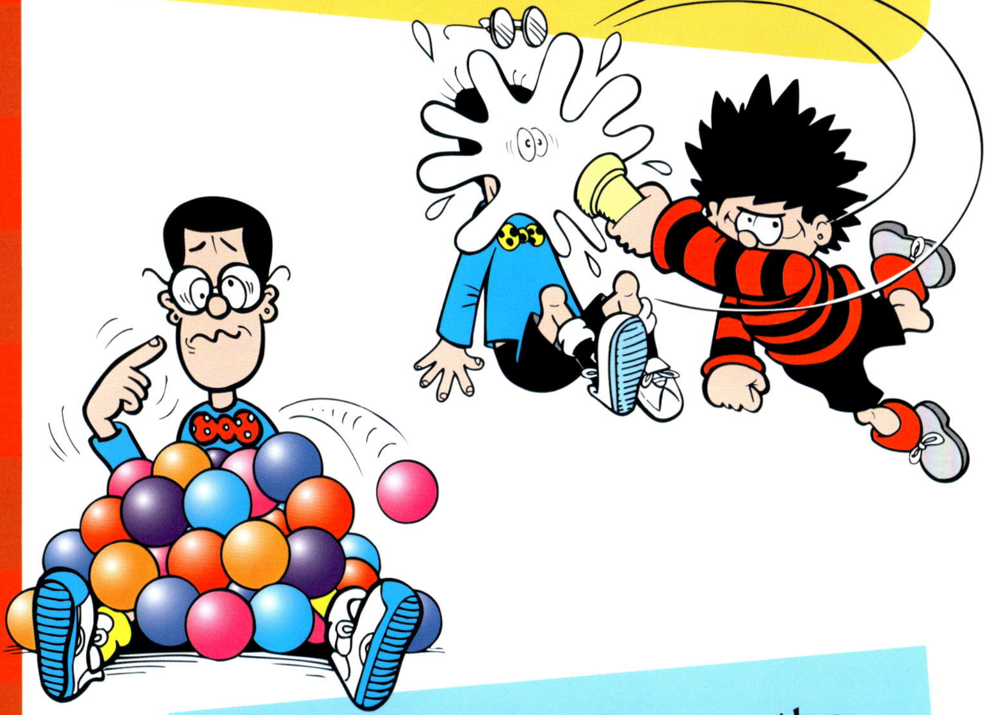

Walter: What game is the smelliest to play?

Dennis: Ping-pong!

What was wrong with wooden cars?

They wooden go!

Why don't traffic lights go swimming?

Because they take forever to change!

UNSCRAMBLE THE LETTERS TO FIND THE FOUR BIRDS THAT ARE HIDING IN THE BUSH FROM THE KITS.

ANSWER

Crow, swallow, starling, wren.

BY USING THE GIVEN LETTERS AS OFTEN AS YOU WISH, HELP BANANAMAN TO SPELL SEVEN FRUITS.

ANSWER Apple, grape, lemon, melon, orange, pear and plum.

PRINT A GIRL'S NAME IN THE EMPTY BOXES READING ACROSS TO COMPLETE THE NAMES OF SEVEN OF DINAH MO'S SCHOOLPALS READING DOWN.

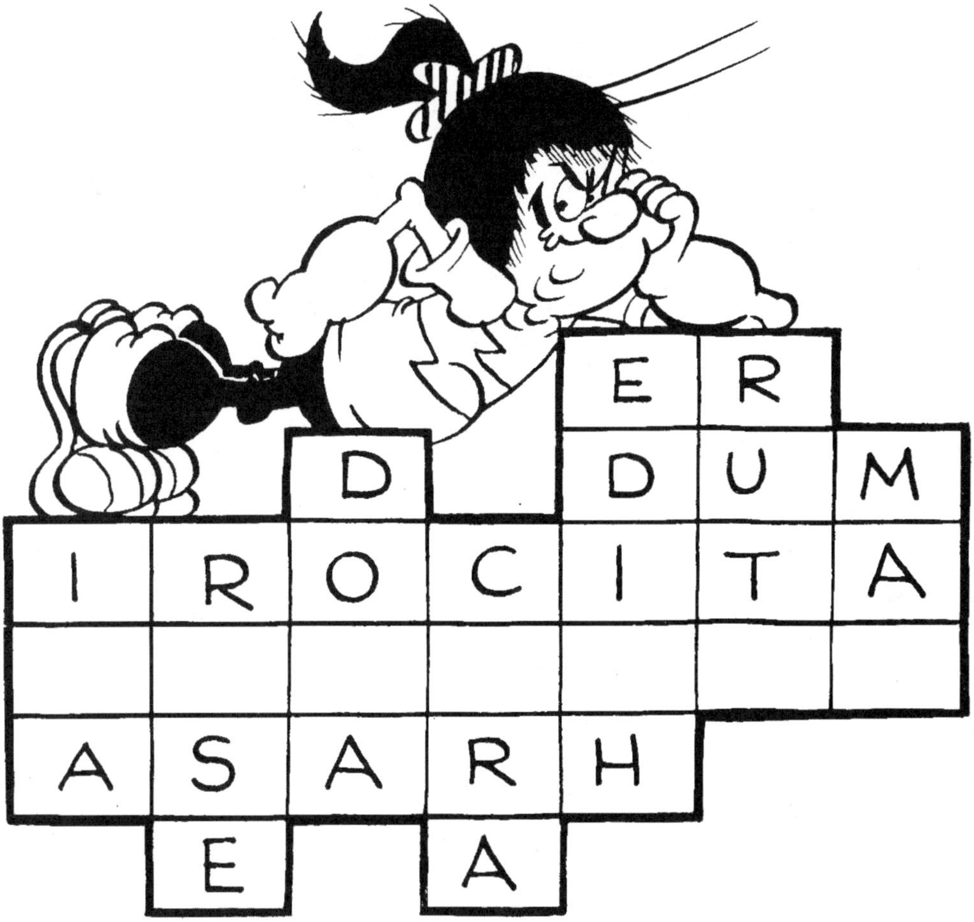

ANSWER:

Write "Dorothy" to spell Ida, Rose, Dora, Cora, Edith, Ruth, May.

ANSWER

Roger's pal is right — the answer is always two!

WALTER HAS GONE UNDERSEA SWIMMING — AND HE'S COME ACROSS QUITE A FEW SEA CREATURES! UNSCRAMBLE EACH GROUP OF LETTERS TO FIND OUT WHAT THEY ARE.

1 BOLSTER
2 SPOUTOC
3 NAEOILS
4 CALMREEK
5 OROSEPIP

ANSWER

1. Lobster. 2. Octopus. 3. Sea-lion. 4. Mackerel. 5. Porpoise.

JONAH HAS HOOKED A WHOPPER HERE! SEE IF YOU CAN CHANGE *CAST* TO *FISH* IN 4 STEPS, ALTERING ONE LETTER TO FORM A NEW WORD AT EACH STEP.

ANSWER

Cast, cash, dash, dish, fish is one solution.

TREASURE MAP
100% RUBBER
N.P.

SEE IF YOU CAN LEAD DENNIS AND GNASHER THROUGH THE MAZE TO THE LOLLIPOPS.

CAN YOU DRAW THIS ENVELOPE BY MAKING ONLY ONE CONTINUOUS LINE? YOU MAY CROSS THE LINES BUT YOU MUST NOT GO OVER THE SAME LINE TWICE.

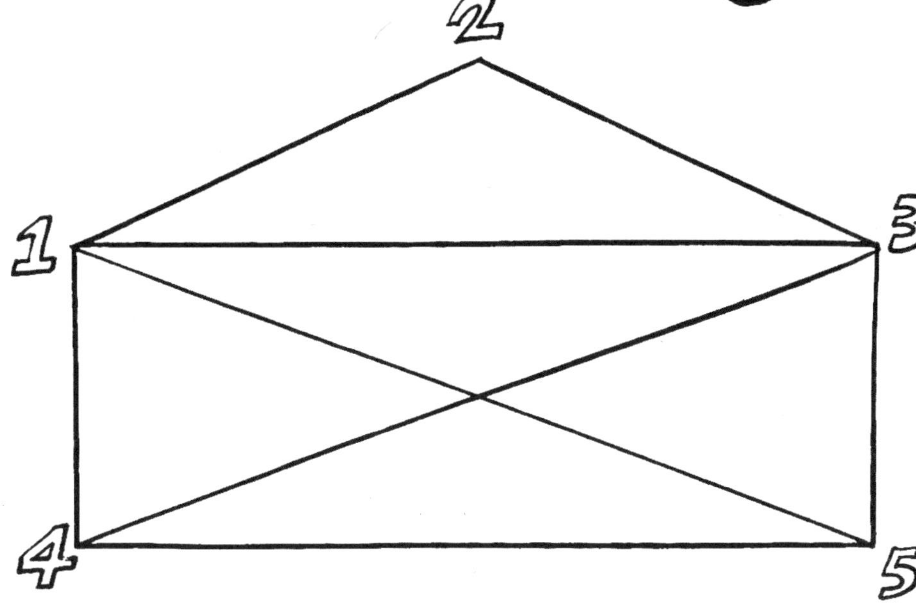

ANSWER

4 to 3 to 5 to 1 to 2 to 3 to 1 to 4 to 5 is one solution.

MINNIE THE MINX HAS COME UP WITH FOUR STRANGE DRAWINGS. DO YOU KNOW WHAT THEY ARE?

ANSWER

A boxing match, a screw-driver, home 'sweet' home and a traffic jam!

SEE IF YOU CAN CHANGE *SOW* TO *PIG* IN SEVEN STEPS, CHANGING ONE LETTER TO FORM ANOTHER WORD WITH EACH MOVE, AND SPELLING THE NAMES OF THREE OTHER ANIMALS WHILE DOING IT.

ANSWER

Sow, cow, how, hoe, doe, dog, dig, pig.

SEE IF YOU CAN HELP PLUG SPOT THE ODD ONE OUT OF THE FOUR OBJECTS DRAWN HERE.

ANSWER

The soldier — he is clockwork. The rest are electrical.

KORKY IS DREAMING ABOUT HIS FAVOURITE FOOD — FISH! BUT ONLY TWO OF THE FISH ARE THE SAME — CAN YOU SPOT THEM?

ANSWER 1 and 5.

IVY THE TERRIBLE'S MUM HAS TAKEN HER TO THE CIRCUS. JOIN THE DOTS TO SEE THE ANIMAL IN THE CAGE THEY ARE LOOKING AT.

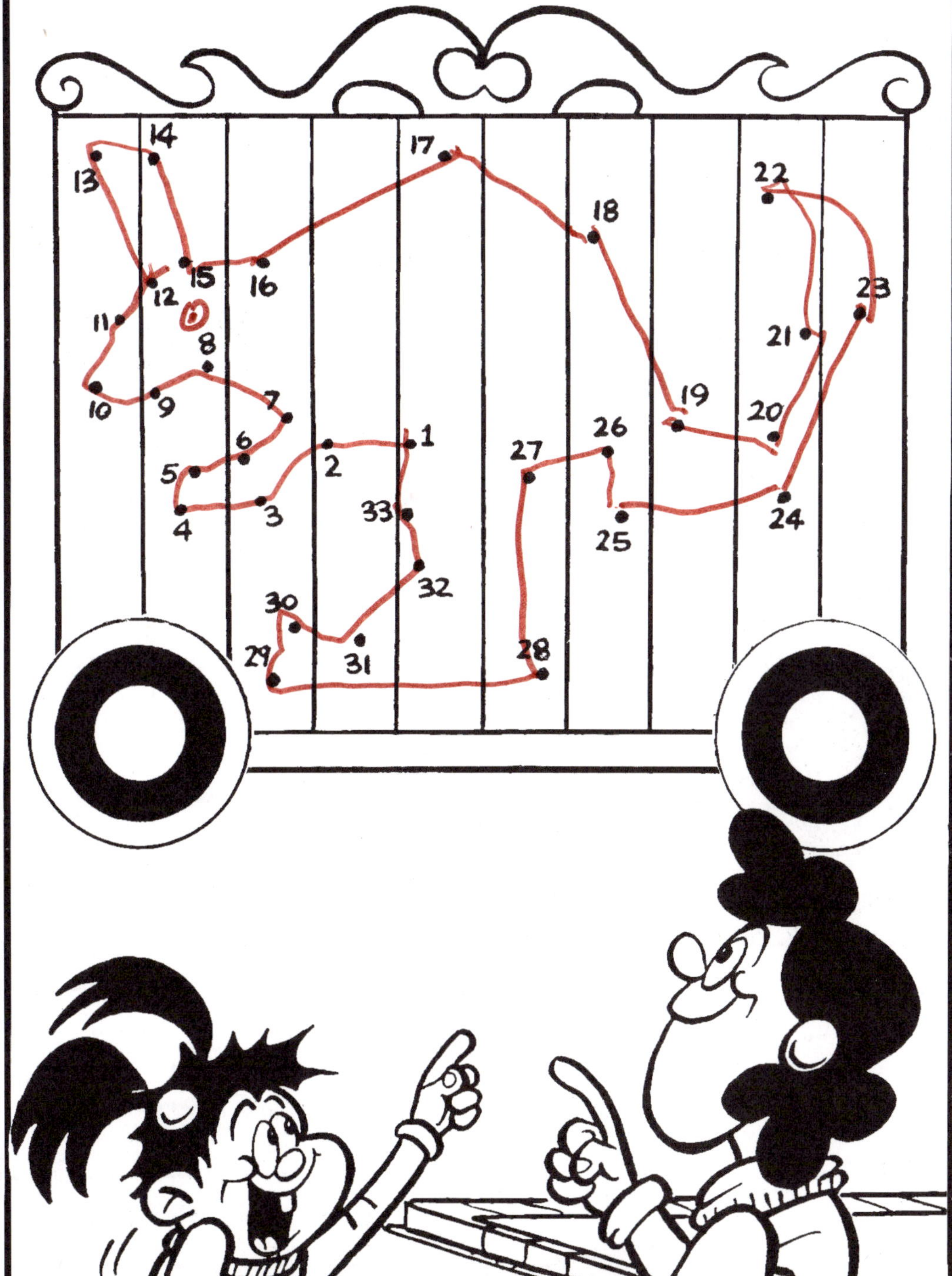

ONE HALF OF *PEAR*, ONE FIFTH OF *APPLE*, AND ONE THIRD OF *CHERRY* WILL SPELL WHICH OTHER FRUIT DINAH MO'S MUM IS ADDING TO THE FRUIT SALAD?

ANSWER Peach

SEE IF YOU CAN HELP SMIFFY WITH THIS ONE — IT'S ALL GREEK TO HIM! REARRANGE THE INITIAL LETTERS OF THE OBJECTS SHOWN TO SPELL THE NAME OF A EUROPEAN CITY.

SEE IF YOU CAN FIND AT LEAST 16 WORDS OF FOUR OR MORE LETTERS BY USING THE LETTERS IN "PIRATE". YOU MUST NOT USE THE SAME LETTER TWICE IN ANY WORD.

ANSWER

Pair, part, pate, pert, pier, rate, reap, ripe, tape, tear, tier, tire, trap, trip, tripe and taper are 16 words.

SEE IF YOU CAN COPY THIS PICTURE OF DESPERATE DAN BY MAKING YOUR LINES CUT THROUGH THE BOXES IN EXACTLY THE SAME PLACES.

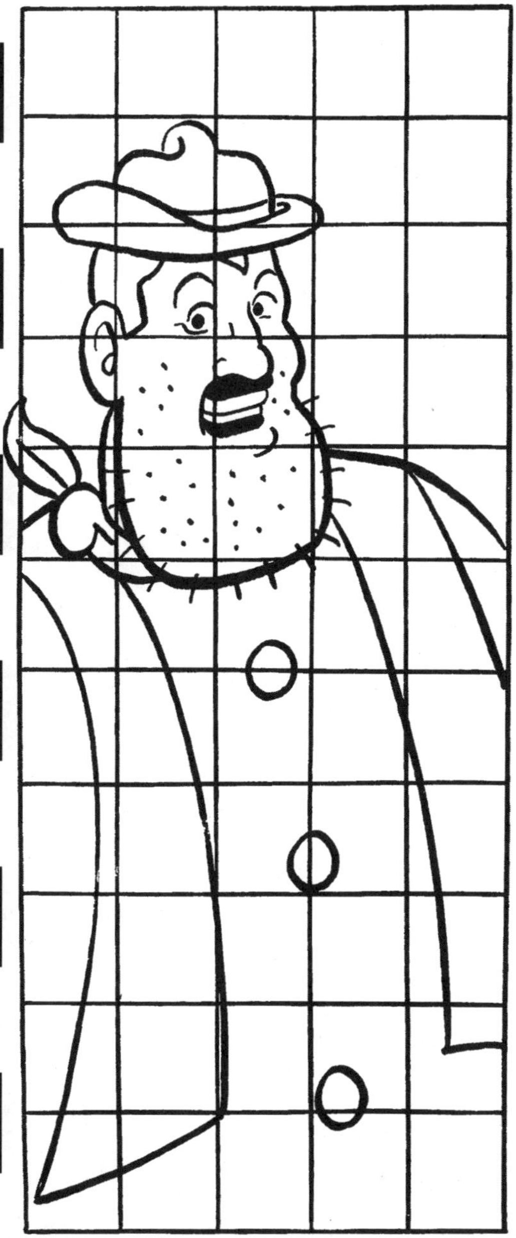

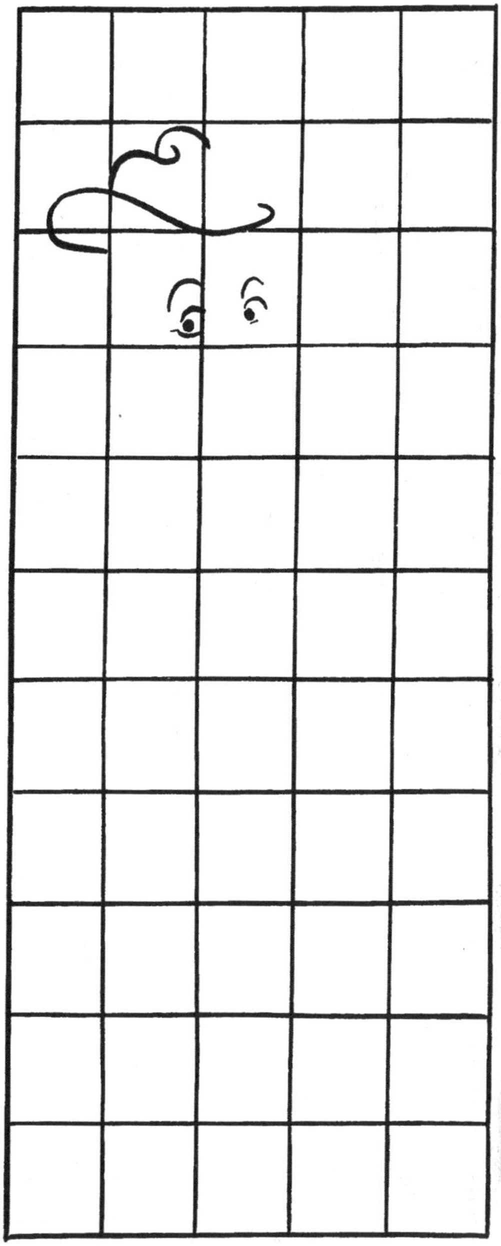

WHO RECEIVED THESE PRESENTS FOR HIS BIRTHDAY? YOU CAN SPELL HIS NAME BY JUGGLING THE INITIAL LETTERS OF EACH ARTICLE.

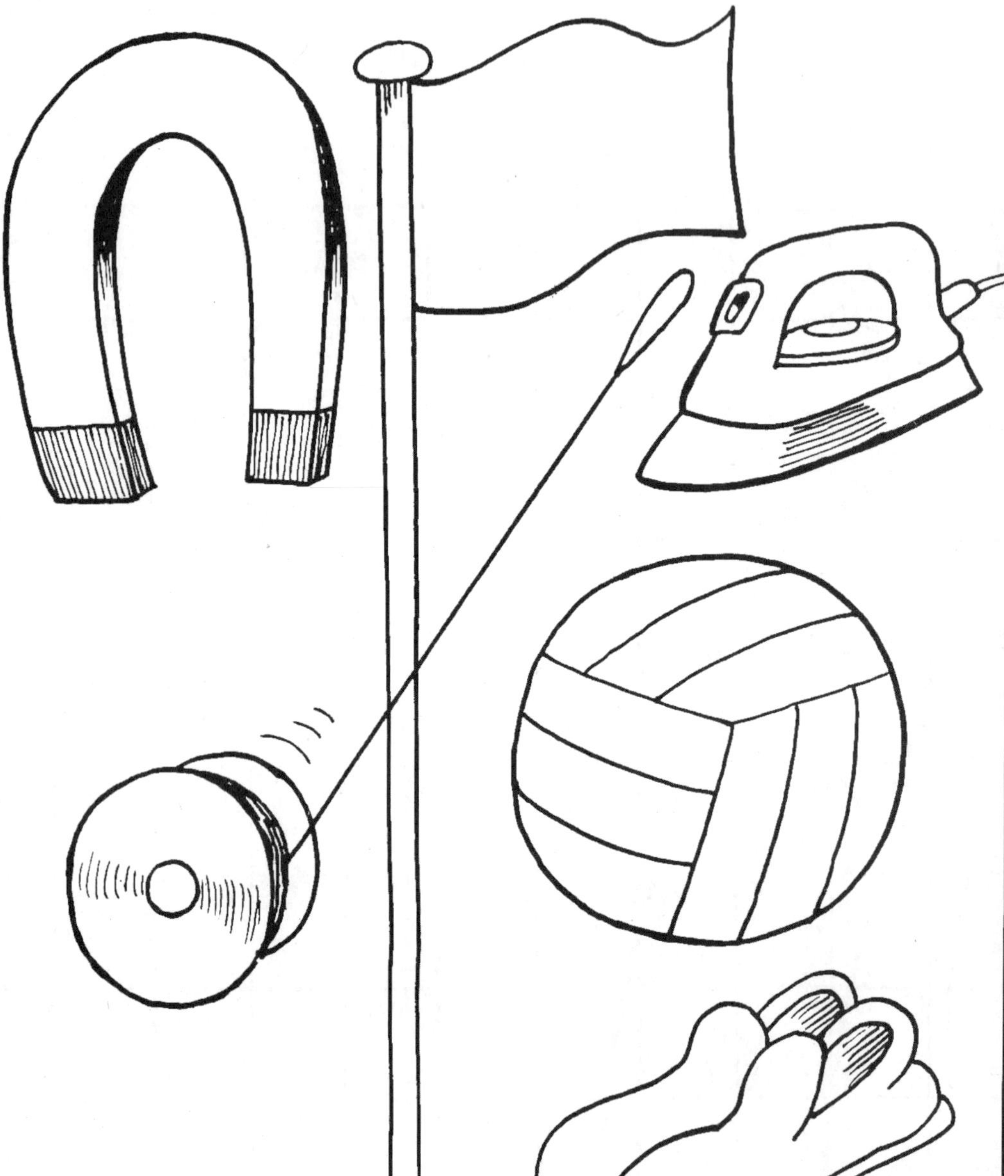

ANSWER

The initial letters of yo-yo, football, magnet, flag, slippers and iron can be rearranged to spell SMIFFY.

PRINT A GIRL'S NAME IN THE EMPTY SQUARES READING ACROSS SO AS TO COMPLETE 6 THREE-LETTER WORDS READING DOWN.
I S A O B H
P T D E N W
ANSWER
Minnie.

BALLBOY'S THOUGHT UP A GAME FOR YOU AND YOUR PAL TO PLAY. STARTING AT POINT 'X', TRACE ALONG THE LINE, TAKING WHICHEVER ROUTE YOU CHOOSE, AND SEE WHO IS THE FIRST TO SCORE A GOAL. IF YOU COME TO A CIRCLE MARKED "TACKLED," THAT'S THE END OF THE RUN, AND IT'S YOUR OPPONENT'S TURN.

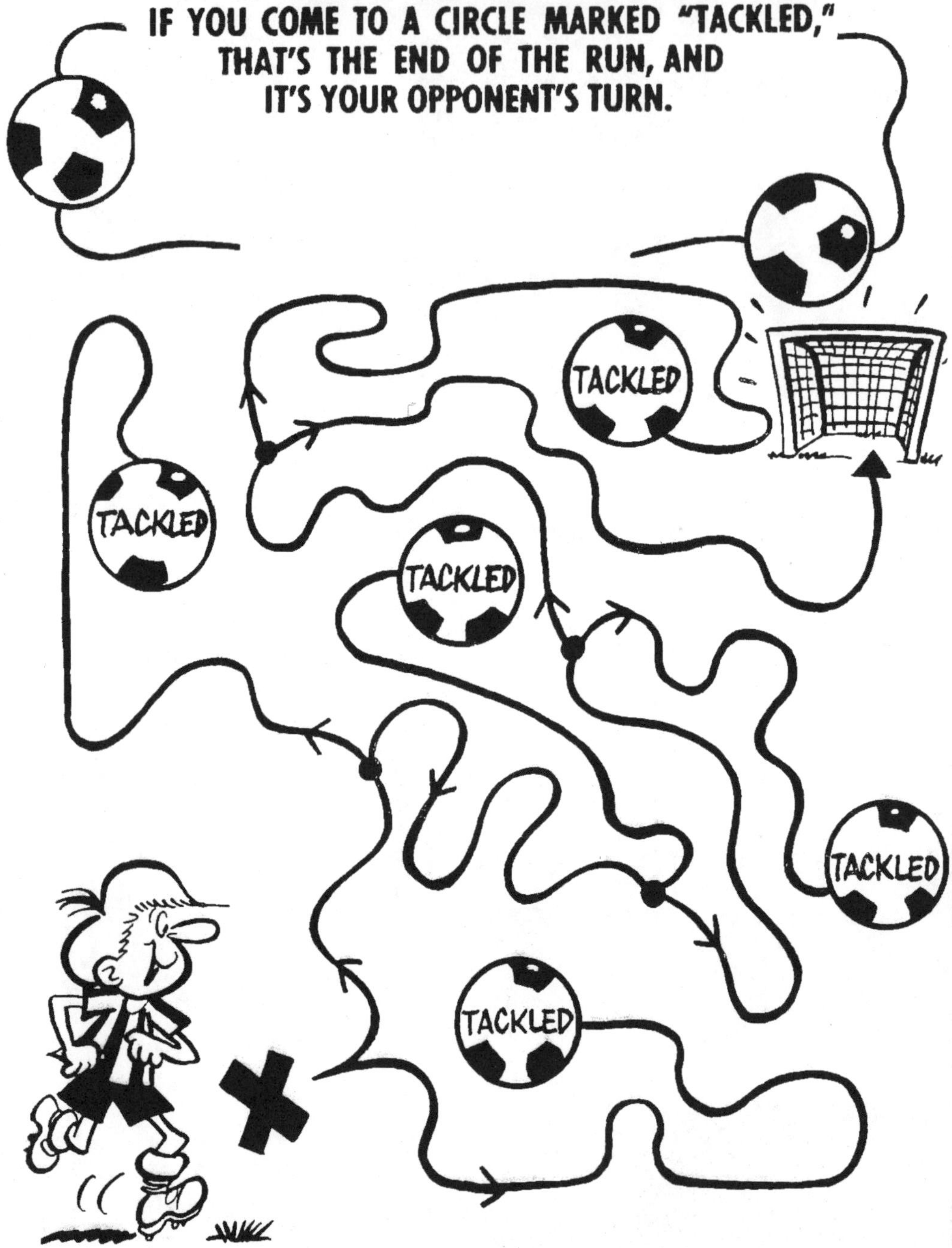

BRASSNECK IS 'NUTS' ABOUT FOOD — IN FACT HE JUST 'BOLTS' IT DOWN! UNSCRAMBLE THE JUMBLED-UP LETTERS TO DISCOVER SOME THINGS HE ENJOYS EATING — AND DRINKING!

ANSWER

Nails, screws, tacks, pins, oil, bolts, nuts.

ALL GOOD THINGS COME IN TWOS — AT LEAST THAT'S WHAT DENNIS AND GNASHER SAY! SEE IF YOU CAN PAIR OFF THE OBJECTS OUR ARTIST HAS DRAWN BELOW.

ANSWER

Sock and shoe, pen and ink, fish and chips, collar and tie.

The cans are piled high, waiting to be knocked down. Using the clues, can you work out the letters which fit in the cans to make a word pyramid? Each word is the same as the last one, plus one letter and we've done the first to start you off.

1. Me. 2. Not out.
3. Writing liquid.
4. Skating area.
5. Thirst quencher.

ANSWER

1. I. 2. In. 3. Ink, 4. Rink, 5. Drink.

DENNIS'S DEN

How soon can you reach it?

Unscramble the letters to find the names of five of Dennis's comic chums.

1. BIZZY WHILL
2. SLEEP TREND
3. THEN SLUM BULKS
4. REPEATED SAND
5. TAKES BRITS SHED

ANSWER

1. BILLY WHIZZ, 2. LES PRETEND, 3. THE NUMBSKULLS, 4. DESPERATE DAN, 5 BASH STREET KIDS.

How quickly can you discover which path will lead Billy Whizz home?

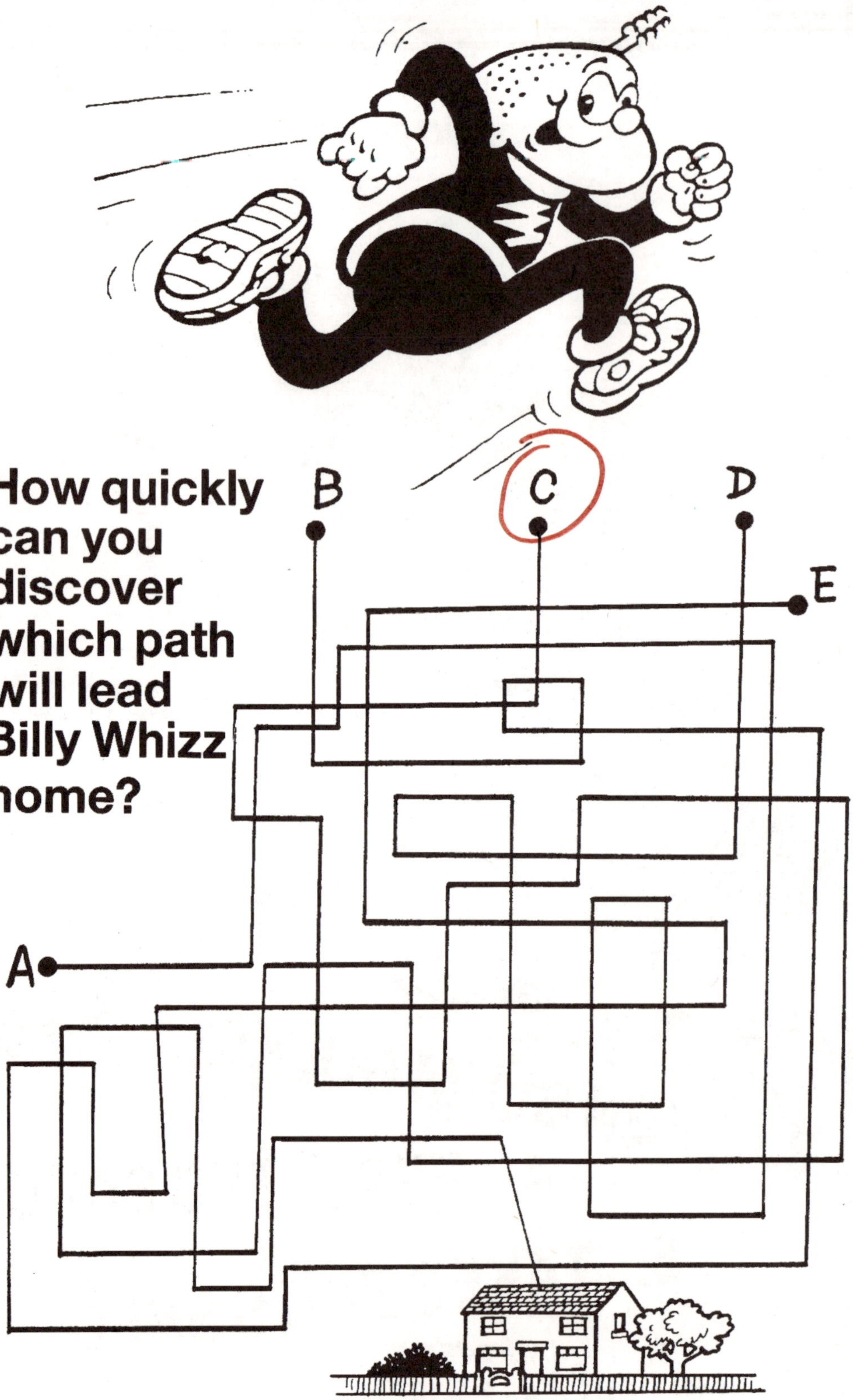

ANSWER
C.

Juggle these letters to spell performers we often see at the circus.

ANSWER
Acrobats.

Copy this picture of Minnie in the empty grid by making your lines cut through the boxes in exactly the same positions as they do in the originals.

Blinky is always getting lost. See if you can help him change LOSE to FIND in seven steps by changing one letter each time.

LOSE

____

____

____

____

____

____

FIND

ANSWER

LOSS, MOSS, MOST, MIST, MINT, MIND, FIND.

Bananaman LOVES bananas, but see if you can fill in the empty squares in the word puzzle and you'll find more of his favourite fruits.

Answers

FIG, ORANGE, PEAR, GRAPE, PEACH, APPLE, PLUM, GRAPEFRUIT.

DENNIS AND GNASHER PUT ON A SHOW!
HOW MANY 4-LETTER WORDS (NO PLURALS) CAN YOU MAKE FROM THE WORD

ENTERTAINMENT

ANSWER

MINT, MINE, METEOR,
MART, MATTER,
RANT, RETAIN, RENT,
REMAIN, ENTER,
NAME, NINE, NEAR,
NATTER, NEAT
TENT, TEEN, LEER, TART,
TIME, TAME, TRAIN,
are some.

Help Ballboy rearrange the jumbled up letters to spell 6 things you might find on a football pitch.

OLAG

LEHISWT

ALBL

ETN

EEFERER

SOPT

ANSWER

GOAL, WHISTLE, BALL,
NET, REFEREE, POST.

Try to think of 8 animals that will rhyme with these 8 words.

CHAIR

HEATER

CAKE

COAL

WAIL

BOAT

HOUSE

RULE

ANSWER

BEAR, CHEETAH, SNAKE, MOLE,
SNAIL, GOAT, MOUSE, MULE.

It's Fatty's birthday. To find out what he's wanting for tea, shade in all the boxes that have an even number.

2 T	7 A	46 R	39 B	17 I	64 C	82 O	51 G
37 C	18 L	41 R	9 E	20 T	13 A	56 R	71 M
41 S	20 A	3 P	61 O	12 L	85 N	31 G	97 E
26 S	83 C	16 R	57 A	62 N	23 K	74 L	95 E

ANSWER

A big cream sponge cake.